Motivating Yourself

Recharging the Human Battery

By Mac Anderson

What does the word motivation really mean, and how does it impact our actions? As far back as Aristotle and Plato, theories abound why some people are highly motivated to achieve their potential and others drift aimlessly through their lives. Simply stated, motivation is an inner drive that compels behavior.

Motivation can take many forms because we are all unique individuals with different dreams and goals. This book is filled with motivational strategies and stories that should appeal to anyone. Use it as a catalyst to refuel your inner drive and renew your commitment to your goals.

Graphics by Balance Design

DEFINE your own Priorities

Everyone has dreams. In the rich soil of our hearts and minds reside the seeds of our desires and potential. What are your dreams and ambitions? What drives you? Let the answers to these foundational questions come from deep within you.

Motivating yourself is critical for a couple of reasons. If you don't choose your own direction, your dreams may waver, and it will be too easy to quit when things get tough. Furthermore, defining your own priorities will also help you determine your future, and prevent others from doing it for you.

Since each individual is unique, it is important to think hard about who you are, who you want to be, what qualities you want to develop and what results you want to achieve. These decisions affect the changes you make and, ultimately, the way you spend your time. By establishing your priorities, you can then make clear decisions and stay focused on what matters most in your life.

"It concerns us to know the purposes we seek in life, for then, like anchors aiming at a definite mark, we shall be more likely to attain what we want." – Aristotle

In many ways, people are more alike than they care to admit. But there is one little difference that almost always makes a big difference. That little difference is attitude. The big difference is whether it is positive or negative.

It has been said that our happiness and success depend not so much on the problems we face, but on how we respond to them. I believe this is true. A positive attitude removes the rust from our minds and motivates us to accept the challenges ahead. It allows us to choose action over apathy, courage over fear, and growth over stagnation. Your attitude will help you find the good in situations and remain optimistic every step along your journey.

Maintaining a positive "can-do" attitude is the key to self-motivation. But your attitude, be it positive or negative, goes far beyond that. Not only does it impact your self-motivation, your happiness and success in life, it also impacts the happiness and success of everyone around you – your family, your friends and your peers. Attitudes truly are contagious, and we must all ask ourselves, "Is mine worth catching?"

"The greatest discovery of any generation is that a human being can alter his life by altering his attitude." – William James

Attitude is a **little thing** that makes a **BIG** difference.

YOU

are in charge

Attitude is everything. The amazing thing about this energizing quality is that it is within your control. You are responsible for how you react to disappointments and what you let influence your life.

A positive outlook allows you to stand up and take control of your life. The following essay by Charles Swindoll is one of my favorites. I've found that it is a great way to recharge your outlook.

> *The longer I live, the more I realize the impact of attitude on life. Attitude, to me is more important than facts.*
>
> *It is more important than the past, than education, than money, than circumstances, than failures, than successes, than what other people think or say or do. It is more important than appearance, giftedness, or skill. It will make or break a company... a church... a home.*
>
> *The remarkable thing is we have a choice every day regarding the attitude we will embrace for that day. We cannot change our pasts, we cannot change the fact that people will act in a certain way. We cannot change the inevitable. The only thing we can do is play on the one string we have, and that is our attitude.*
>
> *I am convinced that life is 10% what happens to me and 90% how I react to it. And so it is with you – we are in charge of our attitudes.*

Discover the MAGIC of Belief

Unwavering and passionate belief in your dreams and goals is the only fuel that will get you over, around or through the many obstacles you'll encounter. Without belief, the opportunities to give up will look too tempting and you could easily take the path of least resistance and quit.

The magic of belief is far greater than most realize. Without exception, the people I've met who have excelled in life are people who believe in themselves and their goals. Although there are thousands of stories about the magic of belief, the following is one I like the best.

For over a hundred years, people had tried to run the mile in less than 4 minutes. In articles written by doctors, all the scientific reasons were offered as to why it was physically impossible.

In 1957, however, a young Englishman named Roger Bannister ran the mile in 3 minutes, 59-1/2 seconds, and made headlines throughout the world.

Far more amazing, is what happened the following year – 47 people ran the mile in less than 4 minutes!

How could this be after thousands of athletes had tried and failed? Well, for the first time, they believed they could do it. As Robert Collier said, "Your chances of success in any undertaking can always be measured by your belief in yourself." In the case of the 4 minute mile, the mental barriers came down, and today, even many high school athletes run the mile in less than 4 minutes.

IGNITE your inner Fire

Passion is the spark that ignites self-motivation. You can't fake it. It starts with examining your purpose in life. We are all blessed with gifts that need to be shared. Some have the gift of creativity, while others are great at working with children; others have excellent mechanical abilities. Whatever the gift, hone your skills in that area and try to become all that you can be.

Rest assured that throughout your career you'll be faced with many obstacles, and the degree of passion you have for your work will shape your attitude toward these barriers. I once heard someone say; "Obstacles are great opportunities brilliantly disguised as unsolvable problems." Was this person passionate about his work? You bet he was!

We're only on this earth for a short time. When our time is up, can you imagine how good it will feel to look back and say, "I am truly proud of what I've done with my life."

"If a man is called to be a streetsweeper, he should sweep streets even as Michelangelo painted, or Beethoven composed music, or Shakespeare wrote poetry. He should sweep the streets so well that all the hosts of heaven and earth will pause to say, here lived a great streetsweeper who did his job well."
– Martin Luther King, Jr.

To make self-motivation work for you, understanding a few key fundamentals is critical. At the top of the list is the need for clearly defined and realistic goals. These goals, in turn, provide the roadmap for you to follow.

In this simple premise, focus on the word "realistic." Why is it important for you to believe, with all your heart, that your goals are attainable? Although researchers on the subject of motivation differ in some areas, they all agree on one thing – the strength of your motivation is directly tied to your expected probability of success. In other words, if you truly feel you can accomplish your objectives, you're likely to be highly motivated. If for whatever reason you feel you may not, then your levels of motivation diminish greatly.

It is human nature to want things to happen quickly. Patience is the key to staying motivated to reach your goal. So while it's wonderful to have big dreams, to get the end result you desire, you'll need to set a series of realistic goals that will take you to the next plateau.

"Have realistic expectations and set attainable goals. Reaching intermittent, moderate goals is certainly more rewarding and enjoyable than floundering amid unrealistic expectations." – Leonard Finkel

Reach for REALISTIC Goals

Make **GOOD HABITS** and THEY will make you

It is difficult to overestimate the value of discipline as it relates to self-motivation. Habits, good or bad, are difficult to break.

Let me offer a simple exercise to demonstrate. Cross your arms as you normally would and look to see which arm is on top. Facts show that approximately 50% of people always place their right arm on top and 50% place their left. It has nothing to do with you being right-handed or left-handed. At some point, early in your childhood, you crossed your arms for the first time and because of habit, you've been doing it that way ever since.

Now cross your arms differently. Place your other arm on top, instead. How does it feel? Weird, right? What if I were to tell you today, that for the rest of your life, when you crossed your arms you'd have to put the "wrong" arm on top. You'd need post-it notes on your hand, your desk and your mirror – as reminders, to help you break that one *simple* habit.

You get the message. Forming good habits or breaking bad ones isn't easy, but can be done. Discipline yourself in the beginning and form good habits that will help you to reach your goals in life.

"Thoughts lead on to purposes; purposes go forth in action; actions form habits; habits decide character; and character fixes our destiny."
– Tyron Edwards

Highly motivated people are focused. Their minds are clear and their energy levels are high. Many things can hold you back from being all you can be. One is "old baggage," emotional scars that continue to linger as giant barriers to your success and your ability to stay motivated.

Many people who have been mistreated or abused never forgive. As much as you can rationalize why a person doesn't deserve your forgiveness, you need to do it any way. If you don't, this refusal can put an invisible ceiling on your future.

Imagine a basketball player with shoes made of steel. After playing the first half of a game in the steel shoes, you can imagine how good it would feel to put on a pair of Nikes and go out and play the second half?

Anger, hate and resentment are truly like a cancer in our body. Just like cancer, they continue to grow unless we deal with them. Letting go of your "old baggage" can immediately give you the energy and the freedom you need to grow. As difficult as it may seem, neglecting forgiveness can be far more costly in the long run.

"Forgiveness is the key that unlocks the door of resentment and the handcuffs of hate. It is a power that breaks the chains of bitterness and the shackles of selfishness." – William A. Ward

LET GO
OF
Old Baggage

Replace

WORRY with

HOPE

A famous physician was quoted as saying, "Worry is the most subtle and destructive of all human diseases. Millions of people are ill because of dammed-up anxiety."

Dr. Norman Vincent Peale in his book, *The Power of Positive Thinking*, says that the first step in breaking the worry habit is simply believing you can. Since, "Imagination is the source of fear and it can also be the cure," he suggests that once a day we practice emptying our minds, and picture all "worry thoughts" as flowing out of our body as you would drain the tub by removing a stopper. After the mind is empty, practice refilling it with thoughts of faith, hope, courage and gratitude.

In essence, I'm convinced we become what we think about, and that we can control what those thoughts are. If we continually practice filling our mind with faith, it will eventually crowd out our fears.

"Of all the forces that make for a better world, none is so indispensible, none so powerful, as hope. Without hope, men are only half alive. With hope, they dream and think and work." – Charles Sawyer

Without question, our levels of motivation are directly tied to our energy levels. The more we exercise, the better we feel about ourselves. Energy can be viewed as the fuel for excellence, and without regular exercise your body's gas tank can run dry quickly.

For a long time I listened to what people had to say regarding the benefits of regular exercise, but it never really "clicked" until I listened to Bob Richards, the great Olympic athlete explain. He said: "Quite simply, exercise gets the heart pumping, the blood flowing, and as a result, gets the 'crud' out of your cardiovascular system." He went on to say that our health is very dependent on having a healthy bloodstream.

During exercise the heart pumps more blood which carries increased amounts of oxygen and nutrients to our cells resulting in higher energy levels. The increased heart rate causes blood to move through our arteries at a faster pace, just as heavy rains create flash floods in rivers and streams. Just as floods cause erosion on the banks of a stream, rapid blood flow helps to remove plaque, or "crud," as Richards calls it, from artery walls. When you truly understand the power of exercise it can make a significant impact in your life and the way you feel each day.

"I think good physical conditioning is essential to any occupation. Someone who is physically fit performs better at any job. Fatigue makes cowards of us all." – Vince Lombardi

EXERCISE to Energize

UNLEASH your Emotional Energy

One of the keys to motivating yourself is understanding your emotions. Our emotions, to a large extent, drive our behavior. The desire for love, recognition, achievement and meaning can be powerful motivators. As the following true story demonstrates, knowing how to harness your emotional energy is the key to achieving a desired result.

The legendary Alabama football coach, Bear Bryant had a young man on the fourth string of his team named Henry Peterson. He had never gotten to play, and just before the Alabama-Auburn game, Bryant got a call from Henry saying his dad had died and he needed to go home.

(continued...)

On Friday, Coach Bryant got another call from Henry and he said, "Coach, I got to thinking about it and I can't let the team down. I want to be there on Saturday."

Sure enough, on Saturday afternoon, Henry was ready to play. He walked up to Bryant and said, "Coach, I want you to start me today!" Bear said, "Henry, this is the Alabama-Auburn game. I can't start you – you've never played!" But Henry persisted, and Bryant, never knowing why, heard himself say, "Okay, Henry, I'll put you in on the first play."

Henry Peterson ran for four touchdowns in the first half. He nearly beat Auburn by himself. The coach walked over to him at half-time and said, "Son, I don't know whether to kiss you or kill you. You've been sitting on my bench for four years, why didn't you tell me you could play like this?"

Henry looked up at him and said, "Coach did you ever see me walking arm and arm around campus with my dad?" Coach Bryant said, "Yes, I think I have seen you with him a few times." "Well, Coach," said Henry, "my dad was blind. Today was the first time he ever got to watch me play football."

Henry discovered his emotional energy, and by harnessing it, produced amazing results. Have you discovered yours?

Don't be AFRAID to Fail

Our reaction to failed attempts at success often determines whether our ultimate goal will ever be reached. Henry Ford once said "Failure is only the opportunity to begin again more intelligently." Consider the following story the next time you fail.

It was late afternoon and a skinny young man was dashing down the steps at his school to check out the bulletin board by the gym. His heart was pounding as he saw the list that was tacked to the board. This list would tell him if his dream of making the high school basketball team would be realized. He read the list again and again, each time with the same result – his name was not there. He had failed. That day, that moment, would change his life.

For the next year, regardless of the weather, he practiced 4-6 hours every day. There were many nights that he was all alone under the moonlight, practicing every move, every shot that he needed to make next year's team.

The ending is a happy one. He did make the team – and Michael Jordan, on the heels of failure, went on to become the greatest basketball player of all time.

"Those who dare to fail miserably, can achieve greatly."
– Robert F. Kennedy

Sometimes the obstacles we face in business, or in life seem overwhelming. For me, the only way to stay focused, and keep my sanity, is to move the mountain one dig at a time.

The first step in resolving any problem is to identify all the things that need to get done. While the list can be intimidating, it's amazing what can happen when enthusiastic people with a common goal attack a problem one day at a time. After a few weeks or months, a faint glimmer of light appears at the end of the tunnel. With that light comes hope, and the belief that what once seemed impossible is doable after all.

While the author of the following poem is unknown, I'm convinced that he or she clearly understood this valuable lesson.

It Can be Done
The ones who miss all the fun
Are those who say, "It can't be done."
In solemn pride they stand aloof,
And greet each venture with reproof.
Had they the power they'd efface,
The history of the human race.
We'd have no radio or motor cars,
No street lit by electric stars;
No telegraph nor telephone,
We'd linger in the age of stone.
The world would sleep if things were run,
By those who say, "It can't be done."

Yard by yard,
LIFE is **HARD.**

Inch by inch,
LIFE'S a **CINCH.**

Persevere

Persevere

Persevere

If someone were to ask me to pick one word to describe whatever success I've had in my life, I wouldn't hesitate – Perseverance.

For all of us, the best laid plans don't always work. Our lives are filled with potholes, roadblocks and detours. However, when times get tough, persisting with every fiber you can muster is paramount.

The next time you could use a little inspiration consider this:

- *Abraham Lincoln* failed in two different businesses and was defeated in 6 elections before being elected President of the United States.
- *Sam Walton* was told by many people that his idea of large discount stores in small towns was crazy.
- *Dr. Seuss'* first children's book was rejected by 23 publishers. The twenty-fourth sold six million copies.
- *Ray Kroc* opened his first McDonald's at age 52, after trying for years to sell the idea of a large chain of fast food restaurants to potential investors.

Perseverance is fueled by passion and your belief that what you are doing is the right thing. Self-motivated people must expect adversity and understand it's a part of life.

"Perseverance is a great element of success. If you only knock long enough and loud enough at the gates, you are sure to wake up somebody."
– Henry Wadsworth Longfellow

How can you excel in your career, be a loving spouse, a supporting friend and a great parent? The key is balance.

In today's world, the risk for burnout is greater than ever. Just as electricity is dangerous when the current is not grounded, you can endanger your job, your family and your well being if the forces which drive your life are not grounded. There is no formula that works for everyone. Each of us must seek our own balance and reconcile our priorities accordingly.

Success is a journey. Your own dreams, attitudes and priorities will serve as the foundation under every step you take. In order to lead a more meaningful life, you need to find the appropriate proportion between your personal and professional interests and balance your individual pursuits with the relationships you value.

"The single greatest element of high energy living is balance; the greater the balance, the greater the joy, energy and creativity." – Ann McGee-Cooper

BALANCE your PRIORITIES

Live with GRATITUDE

Abraham Lincoln said: "People are about as happy as they make up their minds to be." Every day we have that choice to make. Do we focus on the negative things in our lives that will drain our energy and set the "worry wheels" in motion? Or do we focus on all of the blessings that life has bestowed on us? Things like good health, a loving family, good friends, and our freedom to make choices in the greatest country in the world.

Christopher Reeves, following his paralyzing accident, has every reason in the world to feel sorry for himself but he has chosen to "live with gratitude." He's thankful for his family, his life, and his ability to make a difference in the lives of others.

Focusing on what we have, and not on what we don't have, is positive energy in action. Never forget – the best things in life, aren't things. Try every day to show your appreciation to others, even for their smallest deeds. Be thankful for all of life's gifts no matter how insignificant.

"When you are centered in gratitude, you open yourself to all the good that you deserve. Appreciation is the pathway to the heart. It's a law of the universe." – Tim Conner

Each one of us is a one-of-a-kind individual, and we all have gifts that we can share with family, friends, peers and even total strangers. When we give love, knowledge, compassion, or kindness to others, we are giving a piece of ourselves.

It is the act of doing it sincerely, unconditionally and consistently that shapes our character. Our character then shapes us and makes us the person we eventually become.

One may ask what does this have to do with self-motivation. The answer is that positive, motivated people are usually people with a high self-esteem. They feel good about their lives and their ability to share their gifts. They also attract similar individuals who are there for them in times of need.

"It is one of the most beautiful compensations of this life that no man can sincerely try to help another without helping himself." – Ralph Waldo Emerson

Share YOURSELF

the race

"The Race"

Successful methods of motivation, and the behavior that it inspires are as varied as the personalities we all possess. But there are some lessons that seem to have a universal inspirational effect. Of all the stories I've read, "The Race" has made an indelible impact. It teaches us one of life's greatest lessons.

They all lined up so full of hope,
each thought to win the race,
Or tie for first, or if not that,
at least take second place.

And fathers watched from off the side,
each cheering for his son;
And each boy hoped to show his dad
that he would be the one.

The whistle blew, and off they went,
young hearts and hopes afire,
To win, to be the hero there
was each young boy's desire.

And one boy in particular
whose dad was in the crowd,
Was running in the lead and thought,
my dad will be so proud.

But as they sped down the field
across a shallow dip,
The little boy who thought to win,
lost his step and slipped.

Trying hard to catch himself,
his hands flew out in brace,
and mid the laughter of the crowd,
he fell flat on his face.

So down he fell and with him hope,
he couldn't win, not now;
Embarrassed, sad, he only wished
to disappear somehow.

(continued...)

"The Race"

But as he fell his dad stood up,
and showed his anxious face;
Which to the boy so clearly said;
get up and win the race.

He quickly rose, no damage done,
behind a bit, that's all;
And ran with all his might and mind
to make up for his fall,

So anxious to restore himself,
to catch up, to win,
His mind went faster than his legs,
he slipped and fell again.

He wished then he had quit before,
with only one disgrace;
I'm hopeless as a runner now,
I shouldn't try to race.

But in the laughing crowd he searched,
and found his father's face,
That steady look that said again,
get up and win the race.

So up he jumped to try again,
ten yards behind the last;
If I'm going to gain those yards
I've gotta move real fast.

Exerting everything he had,
he regained eight or ten;
But trying so hard to catch the lead
he slipped and fell again.

Defeat; he lay there silently,
a tear dropped from his eye;
There's no sense in running anymore
three strikes I'm out, why try.

The will to rise had disappeared
all hope had fled away;
So far behind, so error prone
I'll never go all the way.

I've lost – so what's the use he thought,
I'll live with my disgrace;
But then he thought about his dad
who soon he'd have to face.

Get up – an echo sounded low,
get up and take your place;
You were not meant for failure here,
get up and win the race.

"The Race"

With borrowed will, get up, it said,
you haven't lost at all;
For winning is no more than this,
to rise each time you fall.

So up he rose to run once more,
and a new commit;
He resolved that win or lose the race,
at least he wouldn't quit.

Three times he'd fallen, stumbling,
three times he rose again;
Now he gave it all he had,
and ran as though to win.

They cheered the winning runner
as he crossed the line first place;
Head high and proud and happy,
no failing, no falling, no disgrace.

But when the fallen youngster
crossed the line last place,
The crowd gave him the greater cheer.
For finishing the race.

And even though he came in last
with head bowed low unproud,
You would have thought he won the race
to listen to the crowd.

And to his dad, he sadly said,
I didn't do so well;
To me you won, his father said,
you rose each time you fell.

And now when things seem dark
and hard and difficult to face,
The memory of that little boy
helps me in my race.

For all of life is like that race
with ups and downs and all,
And all you have to do to win,
Is rise each time you fall.

Every day I hear someone deliver the famous line: "I can never find the time." Granted, our lives are filled with lots of "stuff" but if we were to really analyze all of the non-productive things we do there's always time for our priorities. The question becomes, "Is staying motivated, and constantly moving toward your goals, a priority?" If the answer is yes, you don't have to fight the battle alone. You can find help in three areas.

1. Read Books and Listen to Tapes – There are many great books and tapes offering intelligent insights as to how to stay positive and reach our full potential. Your library should include titles from authors such as, Dennis Waitley, Steven Covey, Norman V. Peale, Brian Tracey, Wayne Dyer, and many others.

2. Learn from Friends and Mentors – Surround yourself with people who are genuinely interested in you achieving your dreams. Winners recognize the need for friends who provide positive reinforcement, and a mentor who can offer insight, advice, and support.

3. Make a Commitment to Yourself – It's a fact, our lives are filled with peaks and valleys and we all need our emotional batteries recharged from time-to-time. Have the courage, the wisdom and the strength to make a conscious commitment to endure even during these tough times.

About the Author

Mac Anderson draws his expertise from experience with three successful companies in the last 25 years.

He is currently the Chairman and Founder of Successories, Inc. which he began in 1988. With 500 employees, over 90 national retail locations, and millions of catalog mailings annually, Successories is the leader in designing and marketing products for business and personal motivation.

Anderson also founded McCord Travel, which he eventually sold to Helene Curtis. Today, McCord is the largest independent travel company in the Midwest, with sales of over $600 million.

Prior to starting McCord, Anderson was vice president of sales and part owner of Orval Kent Food Company, the largest manufacturer of prepared salads in the country. There he received the Marketing Excellence Award from *Sales and Marketing Magazine.*

Anderson's ability to motivate himself throughout his entrepreneurial career is due, in part, to a philosophy on business and life that has remained constant, "To love what you do and feel that it matters – how could anything else be more fun?"